Monologues for Teenage Girls

Susan Pomerance

Dramaline Publications

Dramaline Publications
36-851 Palm View Road, Rancho Mirage, CA 92270

Library of Congress Cataloging-in-Publication Data

Pomerance, Susan.
   Monologues for Teenage Girls/Susan Pomerance.
     p. cm.
   Summary: A collection of monologues for tenage girls, exploring such topics as drugs, blind dates, and having a gay parent.
   ISBN 0-940669-39-0. (alk. paper)
   1. Monologues—Juvenile literature. [1. Monologues.]   I. Title.
PN4305.M6P72   1998
812'.54—dc21   98-21314

Cover art by John Sabel

This book is printed on 55# Glatfelter acid-free paper—a paper that meets the requirements of the American Standard of Permanence of paper for printed library material.

Contents

MARISSA

Even in view of the fact that drug use among teens is a reality, Marissa resents her school's policy of utilizing drug-sniffing dogs. She feels this is an over-the-top reaction, an invasion of privacy, and a lack of understanding of and confidence in the student body who, by and large, is drug-free.

They call us into assembly, okay? And the principal, Old Man Dixon, gets up and says, "We suspect very little drug activity here, but we're letting you know that we don't want it to happen, so we're having the police bring in drug-sniffing dogs. We're also going to remove the lockers and have the campus patrolled from 6:45 in the morning till 3:00 in the afternoon. We're not accusing anybody, and we're not trying to take away any rights. We just want to keep our school drug-free."

Yeah. Sure. Right. Hey, when you start taking out lockers, you're taking away rights, okay? Like your locker's your private thing where you should be able to keep your stuff without having to worry about some paranoid jerk breaking into it. Like just last week they broke into Sally Hume's locker and went through her stuff because some creep told them she was a druggie. Sally Hume? Sally Hume, the straightest kid in school. She won't even drink Classic Coke because she thinks it's addictive. Some butthead just probably had it in for her because she's a dorky straight-A student who doesn't hang out. This is the kind of thing that can happen when people get hysterical and jump to conclusions and overreact. They catch some kid using, and already the whole school's a drug pit. And then you've got people turning people in for nothing just to get even for something. Nazis!

1

And we're gonna have people patrolling the place. Neat, huh? And even more gross, they're gonna bring in dogs. Dogs! What they're doing is turning the place into a prison because they caught some kid with a joint. Hey, like, I know some kids are into drugs. Like, I know some kids drive too fast and get loose sexually and rip off stuff at the mall. *Some* kids! A few. Very few.

What really gets me is that people are taking this attitude that, like, all teenagers are drug-using, out-of-control fools. Maybe they should take a long look at themselves. It's a good thing they didn't have beer police when my parents were in high school.

ASHLEY

Ashley, who recently broke up with her steady, did not have a date for the Christmas dance. Pressured at the last moment, she agreed to date her best friend's brother's friend, a guy visiting for the holidays. Well . . . as is often the case with blind dates, the evening was "unusual."

I knew I shouldn't have done it. It was a mistake from the beginning. But it was the Christmas dance and I'd just broken up with Chad and I had this awesome formal and . . . well . . . I couldn't think of anything worse than staying home. And Doris, my best friend, like, her brother's best friend was in town and didn't have a date, so . . . so why not, okay? I mean, who wants to be sitting around with their mom and dad watching sitcoms when everybody else is out partying?

If I do say so myself, I was totally cool. I had this cute formal with spaghetti straps that was very sophisticated, and shoes right out of Vogue. I was happening. Then Cliff shows up. Did he ever! Like when I open the door, here I'm staring into this guy's belt, okay? This is how tall he was. He wasn't bad looking, I guess. I really couldn't tell, I was too short to see his face.

We get to the dance and everything stops when we walk in the door. Bang! Like the whole room freezes and everybody turns to looks at the freaky couple of the year—Minnie Mouse and Big Bird. It was totally embarrassing. I looked daggers at Doris. She could have at least clued me I was going out with the Washington Monument.

Now for the worst part: When we start to slow dance, I reach up for Cliff's shoulders and I hear something rip—like both of my spaghetti straps had broken. I looked down just in

3

time to keep my dress from falling off my boobs. It was totally mortifying! People laughed. Even the dorks in the cheesy band cracked up.

But then Cliff, who is towering over everybody, spins around and says, "I don't know you people, I'm just here for the holidays, but I'm glad I don't. Because anybody who embarrasses people and makes them feel small is an ultimate creep. Anybody got a problem with that?" Wow! You could have heard paint dry. Nobody moved. Then he says, "C'mon, Ashley, we're outta here."

On the way home we stopped off for pasta at Mama Gina's, where Cliff did all the ordering. Nobody has ever done this before. And we talked and talked and I discovered he was really a neat person—super-intelligent and mannerly. And alluva sudden, him being a giant didn't matter anymore, and the fact that I'd been totally mortified didn't even enter my mind.

He's staying over for New Year's and we're going to the big dance together. This time my dress will be sleeveless.

BRIANNA

Discovering that a parent is homosexual is unsettling and psychologically disruptive. Brianna, making this discovery about her father, was initially devastated. But, with time and the support of her family, she has overcome the problem and, as a result, has become a stronger, more mature young woman.

I'm going to share a very private part of my life with you; something that is very hard for me to talk about, something that I normally discuss only with my family.

My parents separated when I was nine years old and were divorced when I was eleven, an unlikely thing because they never argued and seemed to get along great. But, as I was to find out later, things were far from normal because my father was homosexual.

When I found out that my father was gay, I was, well . . . really upset. I had these feelings of shame, anger, and a bunch of guilt for the bad things I thought about him. And I was worried about how my friends would react if they ever found out. Would they reject me? Would they talk about me behind my back? And I was really concerned about how this would affect the relationship between me and my dad.

At first it was hard for me to visit my father. I had questions and doubts and a lot of crazy ideas about homosexuals. I assumed that all of his friends were gay, too, for example. But, as time wore on, and with the help of a supporting mother and family, I overcame all of this and realized that my father was the same person he always was and that his love for me went way beyond his lifestyle. Our relationship didn't change. And my mom remarried, and I have a neat stepfather. Now I have the best of two diverse worlds.

I still haven't told my friends that my dad is gay because I'm not sure how they'll react because a lot of young people, especially high-schoolers, are very homophobic. When I hear them ridiculing homosexuals it's hurtful and I think, My father is gay, you're ridiculing him. I also wonder how my friends' parents would react if they ever found out. Would they want their kids exposed to homosexuality?

Overall this experience has had a positive effect and has made me the person I am today. I'm more understanding now, and stronger in a lot of ways. I had to grow up very fast and deal with an issue most young people never have to face, and this has made me more mature than my peers. I am more open-minded because I am exposed to the gay lifestyle. I am more open to diversity. I have grown up about what is important in life. And I have become more comfortable with myself and my dad.

This entire experience has had positive effects: I have become more focused on my schoolwork and, as a result, my grades have improved every year. Most important, I'm not afraid to be different and I can concentrate on what I like to do best—dance. When I'm ready for college, I'll be able to carry forward all of the positive stuff I've learned from this and it will help me with my studies, my dancing . . . and life.

BARBARA

Barbara discovers that it's difficult to move outside your circle of friends.

Last week we did this kind of experiment thing, okay? What it was was, we decided to get outside our own clique for a day. We thought it would be a good idea to hang with people other than the ones we usually hang with. I mean, it's one thing to be tight, but maybe by being too tight you lose out on meeting neat people.

My name is Barbara and my friends' names are Bonnie and Blair. We call ourselves the Bs because our names begin with B. Cute, huh? Anyway, we decide to hang with this group that calls itself The Brains because they're super smart—at least they think they are. So I spend a day with this girl named Janice, Bonnie pairs up with Lori, and Blair hooks up with Doris. Well, first off, Janice wants to hang in the library. She loves books. So, I figure, why not? I mean, after all, I had to give it a chance. So we go to the lib and pick out books. She picks out *The History of Macedonia* and I grab a copy of *People*. This will give you some idea of the gap in our personalities. And she really got into it, too. It made me feel weird and kind of embarrassed to be reading about the sex life of the Hollywood Stars while she was brain deep in *The History of Macedonia*.

After the lib we went to the cafeteria. We bumped into Bonnie and Blair and their trade-offs, Lori and Doris. When I looked at them, they rolled their eyes back in their heads. I could tell that they were having trouble hanging with the other Brains, too. We go through the caf and I pick Hostess cupcakes and milk, and Janice puts a bunch of rabbit food on her tray—

7

carrot sticks, celery and an apple. I guess this is the reason she doesn't have any zits. We talk about stuff like school and boyfriends, and stuff like that, and she's amazed that I have this long-term relationship. She doesn't even date.

I can understand this. I mean . . . how many guys know anything about Macedonia?

MAGGIE

At a recent weekend blast, Maggie's friends were drinking heavily and encouraging her to do so. When she refused to take part, she was ridiculed. Since then they have been spreading rumors that she's a prudish square. Confronted with this, Maggie confides to an acquaintance that perhaps it's time to find new friends.

Hey, I think it's time for me to find some new buds. I mean, the way my so-called friends have all been talking about me behind my back. I mean . . . because I don't drink, alluva sudden I'm like this total square.

It's all because of the party they had at John's house last weekend. His parents were out of town and he invited a bunch of us over. Well, they get into his parents' booze and start drinking like they're totally stupid. I couldn't believe it. I mean, they had to drive later, okay? When I tell them they shouldn't be drinking, they look at me like I'm from outer space. They go, "Come on, Mag, have a beer, at least."

I told them they were off the wall and irresponsible, and reminded them of what happened to Richie Harrison—a senior bud who got bombed and drove his car into a van on the interstate and killed himself and a family of four. But even this didn't sink in. Like they were pissed that I wouldn't drink and started to beat up on me with stuff like, "Hey, Mother Teresa won't drink." They called me Little Maggie Two-Shoes. They spent the whole evening putting me down. Finally I got fed up and left.

This week I hear rumors all over school that I'm like this complete square, jerk, nerd, uptight bitch, and like that. And this is from people who I thought were forever friendships,

9

buds I see every day and hang with and shop with and sleep over with.

I know that real friends are like buried treasure and hard to come by, but people who talk bad about you behind your back are better off in your past, you know. So I think it's time for me to start looking for new buds, friends who'll accept me for me and respect my opinions, and not get pissed because I don't want to wind up in a mess of scrap metal on the interstate.

.

JACKI

Many of her friends have had sex, and her boyfriend is pressuring her for sexual favors, but Jacki is resistant. She is not ready to make this kind of commitment. In this speech, she makes it clear that sexual activity is out of the question.

I mean, like, you've got to stop pressuring me, okay? (*beat*) So what? So half of my friends have had sex, so what? What does this mean? It has nothing to do with me and my feelings. Nothing. And besides, if half of my friends have had sex, this means that the other half hasn't—right! So I guess this doesn't make me such a freak after all, does it? (*beat*) Oh, yeah, sure. And what if I get pregnant? (*beat*) How do you know? There aren't any guarantees. Wouldn't that be great. Kids our age with a baby. Do you have any idea what this does to your life? It trashes it. It completely hangs up your future. Are you ready for that for a few moments of pleasure? Or maybe pleasure has nothing to do with it. Maybe getting me to cave will make you feel like a big man with your buds. And that's another thing, how do I know you won't go laying badmouth on me? (*beat*) Yeah, sure. How about Cliff Robinson. After he and Shirley did the thing, he went around telling everyone and now the whole school thinks she's a slut. And she's still dating the turkey. And that's double stupid.

Well, this isn't going to happen to me, no way. (*beat*) Why? Because I'm not ready to make that kind of commitment, that's why. (*beat*) So we've been going together for over a year. What does this mean, anyway? Like there's, like, this time limit on the relationship and after a certain period we're supposed to do it? (*beat*) Well, I'm sorry. Look, the way I see it is, if you really loved me you wouldn't pressure me. You're my

11

boyfriend and you're supposed to care for me and respect me. (beat) Right . . . respect.

And if this means you're going to break up with me, okay, fine. Because what this tells me is that you're not interested in me, you're interested in pleasing yourself and proving something to yourself and being a big man to your stupid friends. Well, *big* men don't pressure girls for sex, Charlie, *big* men are gentlemen.

KAELYN

Not being on the Honor Roll, Kaelyn feels somewhat second-class. But, as she makes clear in this monologue, there is more to life than getting straight As.

If I see one more of these "My Daughter was Student-of-the-Month at Brains High School" bumper stickers, I'm going to freak. I mean, like, it seems like every other bumper in town has one of these billboards to their kids' smartness. I mean, for someone who gets average grades, this is a pain in the butt. Like what would my parents have on their car, "Our Daughter Was Voted Most Brain-Dead at Springfield High?"

Look, I don't mean to trash smart kids, but, sometimes, when your friends are super-brains, it really puts pressure on you with your parents. Like my friend Shelby Flint. She's five-feet six-inches of smarts. It like she's Einstein in drag, or something. I don't think there's anything she doesn't know. Last week this question came up about zoos and she goes and names off all the major zoos in America. Then she goes and throws in that the Denver Zoological Gardens has 304 species and 1300 hundred specimens and specializes in waterfowl and North American hoofed mammals. Hell, all I know about zoos is that they stink.

And Shell impresses the crap out of my parents to the point where they're always busting me about my grades. Hey, like, I'm doing the best I can with the equipment I've got here, okay? Gimmie a break! And, anyway, knowing that the Denver Zoo is heavy into hoofed mammals isn't really all that important to everyday life, you know. Like I'm sure my guy would be really interested in this, right? Yeah, sure.

And, oh yeah, Shelly is very backward when it comes to boys. They stay away from her in droves. I wonder why? She never hangs with regular people. Except for me, most of her friends look like wooden Indians. I guess I'm her connection with the real world of everyday dopes.

Know what? Even though she's super-intelligent, I feel sorry for her. It's like all she has is books. I think it's a whole lot cooler being average and outgoing than a bumper sticker.

MEGHAN

Meghan, a product of divorced parents, is torn about how she will spend her time and how it will affect her relationship with her friends.

Having divorced parents is a bummer. It's, like, bad enough that they didn't make it, you know, but this is just part of it. I mean . . . like having to split your time between your mom and dad, for example. This is a super-drag because it messes up your whole schedule and really screws up your relationships with your friends. You're, like, this in-between person, a human tennis ball bouncing back in forth between your mom and dad. Like last week I had to spend the weekend with my dad over in Fairlawn. This means I have to schlep a whole bunch of clothes and homework and junk. It's like I'm a vagrant, or something, a displaced goon. And I don't know anybody in Fairlawn. All of my buds are here. So, for a whole weekend, I get to sit around my dad's condo and watch him pretend to be young because of his girlfriend. Oh . . . . she's okay, I guess. She's friendly enough. And I can't really blame her for my parents' crackup. They were oil and water long before she came into the picture. But it's just weird, you know, because here my dad's living with someone who could be my older sister.

And when I'm home, my mom wants me to hang with her because I'm supposed to make up for the time I spent with my father. So, here I am, caught in the middle of this competitive thing between them, this game of "Who gets the most of Meghan?"

So, when do I have time to hang with my friends? It's crazy. And I can't expect them to sit around waiting for me while I'm holed up like some a prisoner. But what am I supposed to do? I mean . . . like . . . the whole thing is really bizarre. Here I am, a victim of divorce. It's crazy. I don't want to offend my parents, I don't want to offend my friends, I don't want to hurt anyone's feelings. But, hey! The whole scene's becoming ridiculous. What ever happened to *me?*

All I want to do is live a normal life. But, let me ask you . . . is there ever a normal life for a kid after divorce?

KERRY

Her friends, being from wealthy families, drive their own cars, have money to spend on clothes, movies, and other personal pleasures. But Kerry, due to her family's lack of financial resources, is in no position to compete. Here she displays maturity and clearness of judgment as she speaks of the disparity without bitterness or jealously.

My friend, Doris Eberhart, just got a new BMW for her birthday. Her dad is, like, this big-shot lawyer and makes zillions of dollars. Sally Freeman's father is a plastic surgeon who gets big bucks for messing with peoples faces. She lives on College Hill in a house that looks like a hotel. And Sandra Blake just got a new SUV because she got all Bs on her report card. I got all As and all I got was dinner at Chuck E. Cheese.

Most of my buds have money and new cars and the latest styles. There isn't anything they don't have. And, if they don't have it, all they have to do is snap their fingers and it, like, appears—zap! Me . . . hey, my folks can barely make ends meet. My dad is a driver for Superior Paper Company and my mom works at a dry cleaning place. And they have six kids. So, it just isn't possible for me to compete with my buds—no way. In fact, if I didn't do baby-sitting, I wouldn't be able to hang with them at all.

You know, I've given this it a lot of thought. I mean . . . well . . . about how they have everything and I have nothing. At first I was pissed because I though it was super unfair for some people to have everything and others nothing. But . . . hey! This is the way life is, you know. And when I found out that Doris Eberhart's dad started out working on a garbage truck to

17

pay his way through college, I realized that just because people have money doesn't mean that they don't deserve it or should be hated for it. You can't go around talking trash about people for what they have and being resentful about it, because all this does is bring you down and make you bitter.

Besides . . . my friends are really neat. They always include me and treat me as an equal. They're good people, you know. As for my family . . . hey, I wouldn't trade them for all the BMWs in America.

DORIS

Being an aspiring "star," it's tough for Doris to be stuck in a "nowhere pit" of a town. In this speech, she reveals her frustrations.

Someday! Someday! Someday I'm going to get out of this nowhere pit and get to a real city where my talent will be recognized, where people won't look at me as though I'm made out of pixie dust because I want to be an actress instead of getting married to some brain-dead dork and making a career out of being pregnant. Like my grandmother and mother and most of the women in this town.

Somedays I think I'm going to flip. Just being around people who don't have any curiosity about anything more than daytime TV is super depressing. I see my mom and how there isn't any life in her eyes. It's like all the excitement has been switched off. She goes through this routine day after day, never getting any praise or consideration for the work she does from morning till night. It's, like, here is the hand you've been dealt and this is it, so accept it and don't ask questions, just hunker down and do your ABCs and be a nice little housewife and die. I've asked her about it, but she just kind of smiles this funny little smile and shrugs. Last week when I asked her how she can keep living like she does, she goes, "Your father's a good man." Hey! What does this mean? I don't have any idea. I don't think she does, either. Besides, it wasn't even an answer, it was statement.

When I tell people I'm going to be a star and do plays and movies someday, I just know they don't think I'm serious. It's, like, I'm going through this phase that I'll outgrow. They tell me to get real. And we all know what "get real" means. It

19

means get stupid and get married or get a job at the paper company where, if you're lucky, you get to retire after twenty-five boring years on a treadmill to nowhere.

Well . . . come spring, after graduation, I'm outta here for New York. I know it isn't going to be easy, because I'm going there cold-turkey. But I gotta do it because I think I have talent. Anyway, I'd rather be cold-turkey in New York trying to get a life than dead meat in this stupid town.

SABRINA

She really digs Josh, but Sabrina is not into PDA (Public Displays of Affection). Here she sets him straight regarding her objections to these out-of-line, public exhibitions.

Look, it's not that I don't like you, it's got nothing to do with that. I like you a lot. It's just that I'm not into us groping and drooling over each other for everyone to see. I mean, do you really think this kind of stuff is cool? *(beat)*

So everybody does it—so what? Whoever "everybody" is. Well . . . "everybody" isn't me, and it isn't going to be me— now or ever! And just because some kids are into public displays it doesn't make it right, okay? *(beat)*

Oh, yeah, sure, Doris Wheeler. Please, don't make me gag here, all right? You know what they say about Doris Wheeler. Like she's got the reputation as the school's number-one slut because her behavior in public is so tacky and gross. Like rolling around in the grass with someone on top of her. Hey, Doris—get a room! And like her letting anybody put their hand in her back pocket. What you think they're feeling for . . . loose change? Forget it.

I'm not trying to be a turn off or a prude or anything like that, but I'm just not comfortable slobbering around in public, that's all. And I think you should respect this. Hey, you see how it looks. Kissing in public is one thing, but exchanging body fluids like a couple of dogs in heat is out of the question—totally uncool. I'm just not down with this really heavy action and X-rated behavior.

(beat) So, I'm your girlfriend. Okay, fine. But because I'm your main crush doesn't give your ownership, you know. Being hooked up doesn't mean I come with a title. I'm not a car, Josh.

I don't have your personalized license plate on my butt, I don't automatically turn on when you insert a key, and I don't run on cheap gas. If you think this is what our relationship amounts to, we better get one thing straight right now—this car doesn't run in the fast lane.

GWEN

It all began as a casual evening of fun. But, after a few drinks, the fun escalated to wildness—and then disaster—or Gwen. Here she painfully recalls the incident.

I was the beginning of Spring Break and we wanted to have some fun. So a bunch of us went the Darryl's house to party. His parents were out of town, so we knew it would be a chance to have a cool time. We danced and had some cheap wine. Then Darryl gets into his parents' liquor cabinet and we all had some pretty strong rum and cokes and I got pretty wasted.

After a couple more rum and cokes, I was feeling pretty woozy, so I went off to a bedroom and fell out across a bed. I was almost asleep when I felt someone on top of me. It was Darryl. I said, "Hey, what are you doing?" He said, "Just giving you what you came here for." I tried to get up, but he was way too strong. Before I knew it, he'd pulled off my jeans and panties and had started raping me. I panicked—I didn't know what to do. When I tried to scream, he put his hand over my mouth. After a few minutes, he got up and left and I ran into the bathroom. By this time, my buds, Esther and Sharon, had come in, and when I told them what had happened, they got me dressed and we got out of there—fast! I was so weak and in so much pain I didn't know what to do. We went to the hospital, where the nurses tested me for pregnancy and STDs and did a pelvic. It was terrible.

When I told my parents, they freaked. I went to the police and Darryl was charged with second-degree rape. It was really a nightmare going to school and getting looked at like I was a criminal. Me!—and I was the one who was raped. To make things worse, my case was postponed because the prosecuting attorney didn't think the evidence was strong enough. Then, after I'd appealed, the judge said he wouldn't hear my case because Darryl's right to a speedy trail had been violated. *His* rights had been violated?

I've been going to a counselor and I'm feeling better now. But I'm still pretty insecure and emotional and I cry a lot. In time, I guess, the pain will go away . . . I guess.

KIM

She discovers that learning to drive depends largely on the instructor.

When I mentioned going to driving school, my dad goes, "Why pay out good money for lessons when I can teach you the right way, like my dad taught me?"

When I get behind the wheel, I'm so nervous I could puke. My mind is spinning. Then, before I even have a chance to close the door, my dad yells at me for not putting my seat belt on. Then he goes into this gross stuff about how people get killed every day for not wearing their belts or go "splat" against the windshield like a big bug. Like this wasn't exactly very calming, you know. Then he tells me to start up the car, which I do. Then he tells me to put it in "drive." When I do, the car lurches ahead about ten feet and my dad screams and grabs the wheel and the car jumps the curb in front of our house and trashes my mom's rose garden. Then he starts yelling at me again for being a klutz and then Mom comes out of the house and sees the roses and starts yelling at him and pretty soon they're both yelling at each other and I'm crying. So much for my first lesson.

So I sign up for driving instructions at school. I figure this way I'd be taking lessons from a professional. But this turns out to be the worst because I get Old Man Barker, this major-league geek who wears pocket protectors and space shoes. And he goes by the book. The first day he goes into all this technical stuff about compression and torque and rack and pinion something-or-other and a bunch of crap that has nothing to do with driving. And then there were these two other kids in the car—Jimmy Plank and Daisy Crumwater. Jimmy is a dork who

25

is constantly sucking up snot and Crumwater has enough BO to be declared a toxic dump site. Man, what a scene. I dropped out after the second lesson.

I finally learned to drive from Dennis Black, a cool guy with a new Mustang. He never yelled or got me uptight. He was laid-back and positive and made me feel confident. It's really totally amazing what you can do when someone believes in you.

DARCY

Visiting relatives means boredom and agonizing separation from her teenage buds.

At Christmas, we always go to my Uncle Ed's and Aunt Martha's farm. It's located about ninety miles from here and it's on a dirt road off a road that is off the main highway.

When I was young I used to look forward to going because it was, like, this adventure and different. Now I hate it. So does my brother Zach. I mean . . . what's a teen supposed to do for five days cooped up on some farm in the middle of nowhere with a bunch of people who do nothing but talk about who died last year? Seems like the big, exciting thing in their lives is who hit the wall. And they go into all of this morbid stuff about the funerals and how good the corpses looked. Personally, I'm totally turned off by dead people. And, oh yeah, they like to visit the local cemetery and they insist we go along. Like we're going to be thrilled about staring at a bunch of graves, right?

And Zach and I don't know anybody down there. All of our friends are back in Springfield. So we sit around the house listening to gossip and stupid small talk and watching TV and eating because it breaks the monotony of hearing my uncle talk about far-out stuff like how many pigs he slaughtered last spring. Yuck!

This Christmas I gained eight pounds from sitting around eating grease for five days. Everything they cook is fattening. When I asked if they ever bought bagels, there were like, "Duh, bagels? What's bagels?" They are totally outside people who remind me of the stuff I read about tribes who live in the jungles of Peru. Only difference is they don't go naked. And I can sure see why. Hey . . . I mean, like, seeing them in their clothes is bad enough, you know. (*she shivers at the thought*) You should see my Aunt Helen. She's a tribute to Ding Dongs. She's so heavy, when she gets into her car it sags to the axles. And she's one of the skinny ones. Zach and I call the place Fattsville, Kentucky.

Next year I'm refusing to go. I mean, nobody should be made go to a place that looks like an *X-Files* rerun.

CHRISTINA

After using Christina to establish himself socially, Jerry has dumped her for another. Here she puts him straight regarding his uncool behavior.

Hey, like, whoa! Just a minute, bro. What do I look like here? A bag of ignorant garbage, or something? I mean, after all, it was me who introduced you to these people, remember? They were my friends, and don't forget it.

You come here from out of town, don't know anybody, are lost, unhappy, depressed, sad, wasted, lonely—all of the above, and you beg me to get you inside with my buds. Not that I have, I don't seem to count for much anymore. (*beat*) Sure, right, sure. Like I'm really believing this, you know. Like I'm really believing that you're going to Shirley Anderson's house so she can help with your homework. (*beat*) Hey, don't try to polish your lies, because they won't shine with me. No guy goes to Shirley Anderson's house for homework. And, if they do, they usually wind up in her bedroom getting an advanced course in boobs. (*beat*) What? She's a *nice* girl? What'd she tell you, that she supports her family by selling Girl Scout cookies? Jerry, what do I look like here, cream cheese with eyes? Why do you think they call Anderson "Super Slut?" Why do you think her picture's after the word "easy" in the dictionary.

So what do I get for being nice? What's my reward for introducing you to my friends? I get totally screwed, that's what. I get totally used. I get totally embarrassed. And all you can come up with is some feeble trash that Shirley the Slut is helping you memorize the state capitals over cookies and Kool-Aid. Gimme a break!

29

Look, I'm outta here. I've had it, okay? And don't call me anymore because I'm not at home, I'm out of the country, I'm orbiting the Earth in the space shuttle. Just keep doing your "homework" with Anderson. But next time, remember . . . take along some books.

IRIS

Are the new styles really hip, or are they overstated, overpriced fads? In this speech, Iris raises the question to friend Harriet.

(*Turning before a full-length mirror*) Be honest with me, okay? What do you think of the outfit? (*beat*) Really? Are you sure? Really? (*undecided, turning before mirror*) I don't know . . . you think it's me? (*beat*) I know it's me, Harriet . . . but is it *me?* I mean, *really* me, my personality—does it fit? Am I really the type for bell-bottoms? Don't you think they look kinda dumb? (*beat*) Yeah, like, I know they're hot, but I'm not sure they make *me* look hot. (*beat*) A fashion statement? You really think so? I dunno. I think they make a statement all right, and the statement is . . . "Iris, you look like hell."

You know, I think these clothing people just put out this junk to get our bucks. Like every month there's some new style out and you feel you have to trash your old clothes and get into what's happening fashion-wise because if you don't you're yesterday's papers. And, hey, maybe the stuff isn't so cool anyway. Maybe it makes us look like a clown act. Like these shoes. Who says shoes have to be a foot high? Look at the heels on these things. (*beat*) So everybody's wearing them, so what? So maybe everybody is going around looking like the Frankenstein monster.

I think maybe my older sister has the right idea—even though I wouldn't tell her, 'cause, if I did, she'd beat up on me for admitting she's right. She says you can't be well-dressed if you try to keep up with styles, that you have to go with the old stuff, the classic junk. You've seen the way she dresses. And, as much as I hate to admit it, she always looks hot. The other night she actually had on a *dress!* And she doesn't spend anything on clothing because she shops at these second hand places. But she always looks great. Sometimes I hate her for looking so hot.

You saw how Lindsay Greenwald looked yesterday—awful. And she gets every new style that comes along. You ever see shoes that big in your life? She could barley walk. I don't care if they're in or not, it's not cool to wear shoes that make you walk like a stork.

Know what? I think I'm gonna return this stuff and get my money back. I don't think I need another fashion fix, you know. Hey! Let's go check out my sister's closet. Maybe she has some stuff I can rip off.

RENEE

Renee, like many of us, is not a computer wonk. This is why she expresses great frustration when attempting to upgrade her computer. Here she speaks to her PC as though it were a human antagonist.

Hey, just a minute, what are you taking about here? Whaddya mean, I didn't download right? Don't give me this! I downloaded right! I followed all of the stupid instructions, didn't I? (*fiddles with the keyboard*)

What? You gotta be kidding! What's this "System Error" garbage? And what in the world is "System Error" #875923XRBV, anyway?" It's not even in the manual. (*fiddles with the keyboard*)

Now what? Whaddya you mean, you can't find the printer? You stupid idiot! The printer's right her on my desk. I'm looking at it. I've been using it all evening! Can't find the printer. What's going on here, anyhow? (*fiddles with the keyboard*)

"Insufficient Memory," my butt! I've got more RAM than Dodge trucks. I just installed a zillion RAM last month, you stupid piece of junk!

Do you realize I have book report to turn in by tomorrow morning? And if I don't, I'm in big trouble with Old Man Kramer, the History Nazi. So, see here, you piece of overpriced junk, get working fast! (*fiddles with the keyboard*)

A bomb? A bomb? Why, you cheap clone! There, I've said it, and I'm glad. You're a cheap clone; a cheap, rotten, unfeeling, worthless, ignorant clone! How do you feel about that, Mr. Bomb Butt? I wish we'd never bought you. It was a waste of money. We should have gone for the real thing, like my mom wanted, instead of an inexpensive hunk of crap. God only knows what's inside of you. Probably rusted-out parts from an old Ford. Who knows what you get from a machine made in Outer Mongolia. (*shuts down the unit with an air of defiance*)

There . . . take that, lame-o. You're shut down, baby! You're over. You're history.

I hope you're watching, Mr. Bomb Breath. I hope you can hear me, you nothing piece of trash, because now I'm going to upgrade myself with state-of-the-art no-fail equipment . . . PENCIL AND PAPER!

DIANA

It took Diana months to realize that she was in a abusive, controlling relationship, one that ultimately resulted in serious injury. Here she relates her story, one that is all to common in today's society.

I met Danny in English class. He sat right across from me. He was really cool and funny and made me laugh. Then, one night, he shows up on my doorstep with a dozen roses and this card that says ""I love you." I thought, Wow. This guy is really special. I felt like he was a person I'd want to be with for the rest of my life.

We started going out and, for a while, everything was really cool. We got along great and I was in love with him. Then, like, alluva sudden, like out of nowhere, he started insulting me. He'd say things like, "You're fat," "You're stupid," "You're lucky to have me because nobody else would want you." It was, like, he really got off on calling me names and putting me down. I didn't know what to make of it. I loved him so much I guess I just couldn't think of him as an abuser.

Then the jealously thing started. He accused me of flirting and seeing other guys on the side. If I even so much as blinked at another guy he'd go totally postal. At first, I thought it was flattering, you know; that he was so crazy about me that he didn't want anyone else to have me. Then he'd go ballistic if I wore different lipstick or my favorite miniskirt, or would go out in the evening with my buds. And he started following me everywhere. He said he didn't trust me because I was a slut. Little by little he was moving into my life and taking over and becoming more jealous and controlling.

35

Then, one night, when I refused to have sex with him, he practically raped me. This did it. The next day, when I went to his house to tell him it was all over, he beat me and kicked me and gave me a black eye. I think I had a concussion, because I threw up a lot.

When my mom and dad saw me, they went crazy. My dad called the police and they arrested Danny the next day on campus. This was the end of it.

Thank God I had the nerve to break it up before I got seriously injured and my self-esteem was totally gone. Of course, a lot of it—the fact that you allow yourself to be abused in the first place—has to do with what's going on inside of you, how you feel about yourself and stuff. I realize this now and understand the problem. A lot of girls don't.

MARY

Mary is an attractive girl who takes pride in her appearance. She does not, however, qualify for Miss Boobs America. In this monologues, she expresses her disgust for guys who relate to breasts rather than the person.

Seems like everybody's gone boob crazy. Boobs, boobs, boobs! It's, like, really insane, you know. Especially guys. Sometimes I think they all have between their ears are boobs.

I used to have some respect for Brett Thompson. This is before he opened his stupid mouth and said, "Boobs are great. The bigger the better." A real intelligent remark, right? From a guy who's on the Honor Roll. And I couldn't believe what Billy Whitman said altogether, "Boobs are a lot like a new toy that you play with every day for a week then eventually get sick of." A new toy? That you play with? This just goes to show the mentality of some people.

It seems, like, if you have these humongous breasts this is all that's important to guys. Forget about the fact you're overweight, sloppy, have an IQ your shoe size—this doesn't count. Like Denise Harmon. You'd think her appearance would be a turn-off, you'd think guys would give her a wide pass. But, noooo, no way. You should see the way they follow her around. And why? Because she has these basketballs bouncing around under her food-stained blouse.

Eric Kerns said he'd pay her fifty bucks just to look at them. David Martinez said that if he died he'd want to be laid out between them because this would be the same as going to heaven.

I'll admit that I'm not overstocked in the boobs department, but, like, I'm trim and in good shape and not bad looking, I think. And I'm neat. I don't hang in clothes that let you know what I've had to eat for the past ten days. But are guys following me around like I'm free dessert? Not a chance. Instead they're itching to ring Denise's big doorbells.

I find this disgusting. And *very* depressing.

CLAIRE

A recent transplant from the Midwest, Claire is now living in Palm Springs, California. The transition has been hard because she has had to establish new relationships, and adjust to a new school and climate. Here she speaks by phone to a Midwestern bud.

. . . Yeah, right now it's a 110 degrees. Last night, at eleven, it was still 100 . . . I'm not kidding. Would I kid about living on a griddle? It's, like, I'm this human pancake, or something . . . Yeah, sure, we have a pool. Big deal. Everybody has a pool. But it's way too hot to use during the day, and at night, who's got time to swim? Not me. I've got to study because I've got teachers out here who are homework Nazis . . . I got assigned this book report on *Jane Eyre* that I have to turn in in three days. How about wading through this depressing garbage in this length of time? What am I here, a reading machine? Then, when I finish off *Jane Eyre,* I have this assignment to do on local flora . . . No, I'm not kidding. Hey, you're lucky you're living in Indiana where they're not all uptight about what kind of poison ivy grows near Indianapolis.

And, oh, yeah . . . this also has to be the old capital of the known world. Wall-to-wall old fogies driving around in huge cars at twenty miles per hour. You get behind them, it's just like being in a funeral procession. You know what they call the place? "God's waiting room." I just read where the average age in our community is sixty . . . Yeah, sixty! Just being in the place makes you feel like arthritis. I'm developing senioritis.

To keep from going bananas I'm in a production of *Bye Bye Birdie* . . . So I can't sing or dance, so what? This didn't stop you from stumbling through *Grease.* Anyway, this way I have a change to meet some people and make some friends. And the guy who plays the lead is really hot—like the climate.

. . . Anyway, I'd better hang up. My dad freaks when he gets the phone bill. I'll give you a call next week after I finish with *Jane Eyrehead* and the local flora. Maybe by then the temperature will be down to a nippy 100. G'bye . . . (*hangs up*)

KERRY

Since her divorce, Kerry's mother has dated many men—some younger, some older, some rich, some on the fringes of financial security. Kerry's primary concern is that her mother, if she decides to remarry, marry a man who is loving and supportive.

Since my father walked out, my mom has dated a bunch of guys. At first, my sister and I resented this. I mean . . . having some man in the house other than our dad seemed out of place and awkward. Not that Mom started seeing other men right away. She waited nearly two years before seeing somebody else. I guess when people live together for as long as my mom and dad did, and share a lot of stuff through the years like raising kids and stuff, it isn't easy for them to make adjustments. My sister and I understood this, but it was still pretty weird seeing some stranger sitting in our father's favorite chair.

The first guy was a whole lot younger than our mom. He was very handsome and athletic. He got her into skiing and tennis, which was pretty cool, I guess, except it seemed as though she was going out of her way to be as young as he was. Frankly, I thought he was a jerk. He used to sit around checking himself out in the mirror and messing with his hair. Guys who do this are usually losers. I guess maybe she thought so, too, because she dumped him after about three months.

The second man was just the opposite. He was older than Mom and very stiff and proper. I never ever saw him in anything other than a blazer and necktie. He was, like, this CEO/President of something-or-other and he acted the part. When he'd talk to my sister and me it as like he was holding a meeting. Mom saw him for almost six months, then, suddenly, it was all over. We really don't know what happened, but my sister and I joke that maybe he fired her.

Then there was Jerry, this big Irish guy who told stories that went on forever. He'd come to the house and sit around and bore the living poop out of us. He was friendly and charming, but he was so full of crap it wore you down. Nobody ever figured out what he did for a living or where he lived. It's my guess that he was sleeping in the back of his van. Thank god Mom didn't hang with this turkey very long.

Right now, she's dating her dentist, a real dorky-looking guy who dresses like old movies. We call him Mr. Bicuspid. I don't know what she sees in him. Maybe he's getting her a deal on floss.

I guess after you're married to a person for a lot of years, it takes a while to feel comfortable with somebody else. From my point of view, from what I've seen of the guys Mom has brought home, I think I'd rather stay single. But she has to do what's right for her, I guess. All I hope is that she'll find someone special—like my dad.

ALICE

Alice shows maturity in her defense of a homosexual friend, and great character with respect to the reality of AIDS.

His name was John McHale and I'd known him since I was a little girl. He lived in the house next to us for many years and was a good, special friend. In fact, it seems as though John was always around: at Christmas, birthdays—for all of our special occasions. He was like one of the family—a close relative.

Even though I'd known him since I was a little kid, I didn't figure out he was gay till I was older, till I got a bunch of these stupid comments from some of my buds who made fun of him and said some awful things. When I asked my mom about it, she said that what I heard was right, that John was homosexual. She didn't try to hide it from me or make excuses, or any of that. She said that John was her and my dad's closest friend and that he was a good person—the best. She also told me not to pay any attention to what people—anybody—said, because the kind of people who talk bad about people and put other people down usually do it because they're either ignorant or afraid.

After this, whenever anyone made one of their stupid, ugly remarks about John, I told them to stuff a sock in it, that he was a good friend and neighbor who was kind and considerate and always around when we needed him. And, besides, so he was gay, so what? What did it have to do with anything, anyway? I told them to shut up and get a life. I lost a couple of buds over it, but, hey, who wants these kinds of buds, anyway?

A little over a year ago, I noticed that John didn't look so good. He was usually real healthy looking; tanned and well-built and full of energy. But, alluva sudden, he seemed, like, not to be himself. And he was losing a bunch of weight.

At first, I didn't give it much thought. I just figured he had the flu and couldn't shake it, you know. But, as time went on, he didn't seem to be getting any better. In fact, he was getting thinner and thinner and looking very tired and drawn. And his complexion was terrible. When my folks told me he had AIDS, and that it couldn't be much delayed by drugs and treatment, I couldn't believe it. It really shook me up.

John quit work and stayed around his house. His friends came by and took care of him. My parents were over there every day. They helped with his housework and took him in meals and that. Finally, when it wasn't practical for him to be at home anymore, he went into a hospice.

I went to visit him often. It was really sad to see him. He was very thin and he coughed a lot and by now his skin was the color of newspaper. But he never complained.

I saw him the day he died—a little over a week ago. There wasn't much of him left, just a little bit of the John I used to know. But, you know something? It seemed, like, even though the rest of him was getting smaller, his eyes became bigger and brighter. It was as though they had lights inside. And when, on that last day, when I took his hand, he smiled and said, "Don't be afraid." And, you know, I wasn't, because I realized that he wasn't either.

He was the bravest person I've ever known.

CARLA

Carla is fed up with platitudes and old saws. She feels they are nothing more than statements contrived by adults to avoid facing teen issues and feelings.

I hate it when they say, "Act your age." What does this mean, anyhow? I mean . . . how do you act an age? Like, for example, how would you act different at eighteen than you would at seventeen? There's, like, this huge difference in you over twelve months? You're alluva sudden this different person? Puleeeze! Besides, it's all a bunch of adult garbage, anyway. What they really mean is, "I don't understand where you're coming from so please do what I tell you to do so I won't have to think about it." Telling you to "act your age" is just an easy way of dismissing the fact that maybe you're growing up or hassled or depressed or bored or going through your period— any number of things. Hey . . . it's just another way for adults to avoid getting into what's bugging you.

Why doesn't acting your age apply to adults? My Uncle Richard, who was married to my aunt for thirty years, goes and dumps her from some young bimbo who worked the drive-through at McDonald's. You think anybody said anything about him acting his age? Are you kidding? No way. All the family could talk about was him going though a midlife crisis. What about a teenage crisis? I guess you don't have the right to a crisis till you're going bald or going through menopause. Or till you blow a fortune and your marriage on a hamburger-flipper.

When my dad, who weighs over two-fifty on a good day, goes out a buys a yellow Miata, nobody said, "Act your age." You know what they said? They all said, "You're as young as

45

you feel." The fact that he looks like a bear in a hot dog bun never enters their minds because he's as young as he feels. If I, on the other hand, would go out and get a tattoo, they would say, "Act your age." Go figure.

My older cousin Helen, who was, to hear my mother tell it, the next thing to god, recently left her high-paying job with AT&T to run off to Mexico with her paperboy. The last anyone heard, she was selling her blood to make rent payments. But is her behavior strange? Noooo. Does anybody in the family question her sanity? Noooo. Has a single person said she should act her age? Forget it. Instead they say, "She's looking for new horizons." Can you believe it? Running off with your paperboy and living in a lean-to without running water is looking for new horizons, but if I buy a push-up bra, I'm not acting my age. Wow!

I think the next time my mom spends a fortune on plastic figurines from Home Shopping, or tries to squeeze her buns into a size-five mini, or cries over one of her soaps, I'll say, "Act your age." And the next time she tells me to act my age, I'll tell her, "I'm looking for new horizons."

Oh, by the way . . . we got a letter from my cousin Helen yesterday. The paperboy dumped her for an older woman.

SHARON

An act of physical violence has awakened Sharon to the negative effects of drinking.

It was a teachers' holiday, and Tim's folks were out of town for the weekend, so we had the place all to ourselves. So Tim invites a bunch of us over; there must have been twenty of us. We ordered in pizza and stuff. Then Tim broke out the booze and we got into it and, after a while, we were loose and dancing and listening to sounds and really partying.

Most of the time Tim's an okay guy. Except when he drinks, that is. When he gets loaded he's, like, well . . . a different person altogether—aggressive and loud and out of control. He's the kind of person who should never take a drink.

Anyway, we're all partying and kicking and having a good time when we notice that Tim isn't anywhere in sight. At first, we figured he'd gone off to the bathroom, or something. But, after a while, when he hadn't returned, we got worried. Maybe he was sick from all of the alcohol. So we go checking for him.

We checked out the garage, the backyard, all the rooms downstairs, even the basement. Then we go upstairs. When we get to his parents' bedroom, the door's locked. When we pounded on it, Tim told us to go away. Then we hear a girl scream. Knowing what Tim's like when he's drunk, I knew there was big trouble. We pounded and yelled at him, but he still won't open up.

Finally, I ran downstairs and got Bob Marshall, who's a tackle on the football team and strong as a horse. When he breaks the door open, we see Tim with Robyn Graham. He's on top of her. Marshal pulled him off and slapped him around and I got Robyn out of there fast.

Robyn is pressing charges and the story's all over town. If Tim loses he could go be in deep do-do. And my parents have grounded me for a month for being at a party where there was no adult supervision. They're really mad. As they should be. I should have known better.

And as for drinking . . . I've come to the conclusion that the only good place for alcohol is down your kitchen sink.

LOIS

Fed up with Carl's unattractive behavior, Lois finally levels.

I'm not going with you to any more stupid parties, Carl, forget about it. Besides, why would I want to go with someone who's a spoiled, self-centered, rich brat, who's full of a bunch of silly crap about his family and their money and what a great athlete and brain he is? The last time we dated, this is all I heard for hours—in the car, even in the movie. You kept it up all though the picture. Why do you think I had you buy three tubs of popcorn? To keep your big mouth full, that's why.

Do you have even the slightest idea how much you brag? And, when you're not bragging, you're putting people down— everybody. Seems like all your buds are jerks or ugly or mental midgets, or don't know how to dress. Like you're so damned perfect. Like you're so beautiful. Like you're so styled-out. Like you're so much better than everybody else. Like you're *God!*

And you wonder why nobody can stand you? Hello! Hello! Bells are ringing! It's all over the front page! This doesn't take a lot of thinking, Carl. Nobody can stand you because you're such a stuck-up, egoed-out jerk. You ever take a good look at yourself? Try it sometime, okay? Take a good look at the mess you are. You're a living train wreck, Carl, a condemned house, an unmade bed.

I got it. Why don't you take yourself to the party. It'll be the perfect date—You and You. The perfect couple, perfectly suited, perfectly matched, perfectly perfect. Just think what a wonderful time you'll have with yourself. You can brag and bitch and make fun of people and You'll agree with You on everything. And neither of you will be bored because you're boring people.

You know what your problem is, Carl? Your problem is that your parents goofed you up by giving you everything you ever wanted from the time you could walk: Clothes, cars, money— you name it. You've got your own boat, your own motorcycle, your own BMW. You're the only person I know who owns a horse.

Know what, Carl? Instead of your dad giving you everything you ever wanted, he should have taken you out behind the stable and kicked some serious butt.

FRAN

Fran's boyfriend, Dan, has an insatiable appetite. No only does she find his appetite excessive, she also is put off by his poor table manners. Here she complains to a bud:

Mary, eating with Dan is like eating with a wolf. Maybe a wolf pack. You've never seen anybody eat like this in your entire life. He never gets enough. We go out, he orders *everything*. Last night, after the movie, we go to Jimmy's for a bite. Just a bite, a snack, okay? But, no, with him it's never a snack, it's always garbage time.

We sit down . . . I order a large Pepsi. When the guy asks Dan what he wants, he can't tell him because he's still going over the menu like it's a book he has to memorize for a test, or something. Finally, after mulling over the thing for five minutes, he rattles off his order: a vanilla milkshake, a large order of fries, an order of onion rings, a double cheeseburger with mushrooms, bacon, peppers and three kinds of cheese, and a piece of pecan pie à la mode—two dips. The waiter had trouble getting it all down because the poor guy didn't take shorthand. What a scene. It was very embarrassing. Mary, having your date turn into a pig right before your eyes is not a pleasant sight.

Now here comes the meal. They bring it in on a forklift. In front of him are the Himalayas and he's ready to climb. Now Dan doesn't just eat—he devours. Watching him eat is like going to see *Jaws*. He digs into this pile of gook with both hands. Forget about forks. So he can get more milkshake, he uses four straws. Then he goes and dumps globs of catsup on his fries till they look like they're bleeding to death. Then he proceeds to eat them with his fingers. It was like watching an episode of *ER*. (*she shivers*)

And, oh yeah, get this: He eats his pie right along with his burger and fries. And he talks all the time he's eating so you've got cheeseburger-pecan à la mode in your face. And he ate everything and then wiped his place with a piece of bun. It was disgusting.

Then, on the way home, he wants to stop off for a taco. Can you believe it? I don't know how much longer I can take it, Mary. Too bad he's so damn buff.

VANESSA

She has lost patience with her father's alcoholic behavior. In this scene she finally lashes out, admonishing him for his irresponsible, abusive nature.

What? . . . (*beat*) No! I don't wanna hear it! I don't wanna hear your problems and complaints and how the world's against you, understand? I've had it with this. okay? I'm fed up with your excuses and sob-stories because they're total bullshit. (*beat*) Yeah, you heard me right . . . total bullshit! (*beat*)

Why shouldn't I talk to my father this way? Give me one good reason why I shouldn't. (*beat*) Because I should respect you? Give me one good reason why I should? (*beat*) Because you're my father? C'mon, get real here. This is a joke, man. Since when have you ever been a father or husband or a responsible person we could look up to? Since when have you ever been anything to anybody but yourself? Since when have you ever cared about anybody else, about what they think or feel? You go out of your way to step on people's feelings. You step on them and wipe your feet on them and walk away. You're not a father. You're not a husband. You're nothing. You're a joke!

Look at you. Just look at yourself. You look like a derelict. Where'd you sleep last night, in a dumpster? If you had any respect for yourself or your family, you wouldn't let us see you like this. You're a bum, man, a bum! (*beat*) Yeah, and I'm really scared, can't you tell? Like, I'm really shaking like a plate of Jell-O here. Hey, your threats won't work with me . . . I'm not Mom here, man, I'm not a pitiful little person you can slap around, understand? You take a swing at me, and I don't care if you're my father or not, I'll. . . . And that's another

53

thing, and this is the worst, most sickening thing of all. It's one thing to be a weak, drunken, irresponsible joke who's a disgrace to his family, who blames his problems on the world, but it's another when you start pushing people around. Like Mom. My mother. And all she's ever done is make excuses for you and try to hold the family together. If it wasn't for her, there wouldn't be a family.

Let me tell you something, okay? And I want you to try to get this into your rum-soaked head . . . If you ever so much as lay a finger on her again, you'll be buried so deep in jail they'll have to dynamite to find you.

Now do us all a favor and get out of our lives.

BERTHA

Bertha loves to hear her grandmother speak of the past, realizing that her stories are an important connection to her heritage.

Tell me again, Grandma. Tell me about the old times. Tell me the times when you were a young girl growing up on a farm back in Indiana. Tell me about your friends and family and the people in your town. Tell me again, okay?

Tell me about the land and the crops and what people did before there were computers and all of the technology we have today. Tell me about your school and your teachers and your studies and the kids you went to school with. How was it growing up way back then? What was it like being so far away in a little house in a little corner of America? How did you spend your time? What was the weather like? Tell me again, Grandma.

Tell me all about the summers and the things you did to pass the time. Did you play games? What kind of games did you play? What did you do on the Fourth of July? Were there fireworks and bands and parades? Tell me again about the birthdays with homemade cake and homemade ice cream and how, because you couldn't afford presents, you got a hug for every year. Tell me again.

Tell me about the harvesting of the wheat and how the neighbors came to help with the work and the big dinner the women cooked. Tell me about the creek that ran beside your house and how you could hear it when you slept. And, oh yeah, tell me about Memorial Day, or, as you used to call it, Flag Day, because this was the day you decorated the graves. What about the people in the graves? How many had been relatives?

How many had been friends? Tell me about Thanksgiving and the family and the food and the conversation around the dinner table. Did Great Grandfather carve the turkey? Did anyone say grace? Tell me more about Grandfather and how you met. Tell me about your life together and about your first home and your babies—my mom and uncles and aunts. Tell me again.

Talk about the winters and the cold nights and the log fires and the popcorn and apples. Tell me again all about Christmas and about going to Fox Hollow to cut the tree on Mr. Congrove's farm. Tell me about the homemade ornaments and real candles and the angel Aunt Ruth made from old curtains. And don't forget about Christmas Eve and going to church, where you were given a special treat—a tangerine. Tell me these stories even if I've heard them before. I don't mind because I love them. So tell me, Grandma, tell me again.

JOANNA

Even though Joanna's best bud's behavior has upset her many times, she has, out of respect for their friendship, overlooked the indiscretions. But her last act of allowing random dates into her home is too much to tolerate.

Look, Cindi, it's one thing that you trash my CD collection. I can handle this, okay? Even though you did trash my coolest sounds. Like, in case you'd like to know, it cost me over a hundred bucks to replace the stuff. And I didn't say anything when you borrowed my favorite suede jacket and brought it back with coffee stains all over it. You could have at least had it cleaned. And when you tried to steal my main crush, did I get crazy? No. I was cool, even though it really hurt me a lot to think you'd try to get next to Jerry behind my back. Most people would have shut you down right then. And how about the time you went out and bought the same dress I'd bought for our Spring formal. You think this was cool, you think this was a nice thing to do? There's just no way you should have done this. But did I say anything? Did I totally freak? No. Even though I was very disappointed, I stayed mellow because we were best buds. I've always tried to keep it together between us, even though you've done some far-out stuff. But now, like, this time, you've really gone outside the lines big time.

Look, when you called me the week my mom and I were going out of town and asked me if you could hang at our place because you weren't getting along with your parents, I didn't hesitate because I knew you were stressed, because I believed you needed help. I went right to my mom and told her the scene and she said it was cool. So I give you the keys to our house. This is trust, Cindi, trust big time.

And what do you do with this trust? Did you respect it? Do you behave like a guest should in someone else's home? No, no way—you go and blow it! When we come back we find the place totally trashed, everything upside down, stuff broken because you brought people in to party. (*beat*) Don't lie to me, Cindi. Jason Evers said you partied every night. He said one night it was so loud the neighbors called the cops.

And this isn't the worst part of it, you little slut! The worst part is, I find out you fooled around with random dudes in my bedroom. And you gave out my phone number to them, you fool. (*beat*) The hell you didn't, bitch! I'm getting raunchy phone calls every night from these guys. Do you have any idea how sickening this is? Do you know how disgusting it is for me to know that you used my bed as your playpen? So, consider us history, Cindi. It's over, okay? Don't call me. Nothing. And when we pass each other in the halls, don't speak. I don't want anybody seeing me talking with trash.

MAE

She is on the phone with her best bud, describing an encounter with . . . well, let the monologue tell the story:

(*into receiver*) I ran into him at Barnes & Noble. He didn't say, "Hi," Hello," "How are you," "Nice day," nothing like this. The first thing he says to me, right out of the blue, is, "You're born, you struggle, and then you die." (*beat*) Right. He actually said this. Is this off-the-wall, or what? (*beat*) I know, you just don't hear opening lines like this every day. He was totally different from anyone I've ever met. And he was different looking, too. Had this real intense stare and hair that looked like it'd been cut with hedge trimmers. And, oh yeah, he had a goatee. How many guys do you know with a goatee? (*beat*) Right, not any. And he was wearing this beat-up old corduroy jacket and a pair of wire-rimmed glasses with one of the stems held on with a straight pin. He was strange, totally different. And not bad looking. He was kinda handsome, actually.

Anyway, here I was, browsing through the magazines, checking out the fan mags, when he walks up carrying seven tons of poetry. He wanted to know if I'd ever read *On the Road*. When I asked him if it was published by the Auto Club, he got this funny look around the mouth like he'd just swallowed Liquid Plumber. Hey, I was serious. Then he asked me if I'd ever read *War and Peace*. When I said why would I want to waste my time reading it when I could rent the video, he got this funny look again.

Then he asked me if I'd like to have lunch, and I accepted. Ordinarily, I'd never do anything like this, but this dude was so different, I just couldn't resist. So we go to this health-food place, The Raging Lettuce, over on Fourth Street. Of course, he's a strict vegetarian, so he orders up this concoction made up of carrots and spinach and seaweed and junk that they grind up in a blender. When they pour it out, it looks like gremlin barf. There wasn't a cheeseburger in sight, so I ordered a salad that looked and tasted like hay. Awful.

During lunch, he goes on and on about Shakespeare and Yates and Dylan Thomas. His name was Dylan, by the way. Figures, right? And the only films he liked were foreign. He loved subtitles. Said they were pure. When I asked him how he could read the subtitles and watch the picture at the same time, he didn't have an answer. When the waitress brought the check, he said to her, "You're born, you struggle, and then you die." This is when I excused myself to go to the ladies' room. Instead, I left the poet with his vomit milkshake.

I'm staying out of Barnes & Noble.